Manipulation Tips And Tricks

A Modern Guide To Master The Art Of Persuasion, Power,
Manipulation, Negotiation, Deception, And Psychological Warfare

Adam Smith

Manipulation Tips And Tricks

Table of Contents

Manipulation Tips And Tricks

Introduction

There is usually a person who may enter in an area full of people and in just a short time, describe with precision, the relationship that exists between these people and their emotional states.

The reading ability the individual's attitudes as well as their thoughts based on their behavior use to be the initial system of communication that humans used long before the evolution of verbal language.

Years before the invention of the radio, communication was carried out through writing newspapers, books, and letters. This implied that poor speakers and politicians could do just fine in their careers if they kept at it long enough and produced a good printed copy.

To be able to understand what is really going on in a person's life is a bit difficult. It mainly entails analyzing whatever you hear and see within the surrounding where ¬everything happens. Once that has been done, the next thing would be to draw possible conclusions.

However, a majority of people only see the things that they believe they are seeing. At times, we tend to say that we know certain things 'like the back of our hand'. This quote is not accurate. According to recent studies, just about 5% of people can recognize the back side or dorsal surface of their hands from a photograph.

In this e-book, you will learn some of the best ways of deciphering body language. In addition to that, you will also be able to break down several other fears, attitudes, and beliefs, and get to understand the underlying force that is behind some of the actions that people undertake.

Chapter 1:

Analyzing People Through the Nonverbals of the Hands and the Palms

Whereas the key to success when it comes to both professional and personal relationships lies in the ability to communicate correctly, it is not necessarily the words that one uses but the body language and nonverbal cues that speak volumes.

Hiding behind a barrier is one of the typical responses that we learn at a tender age. We usually do this as a way of offering protection to ourselves.

As kids, it was reasonable to hide behind particular solid objects like furniture whenever we realized that we had gotten into hot soup or threatening situations.

As we continue to advance in age, this behavior of hiding becomes sophisticated, as just another behavior pops in. Since hiding behind an object was one of the prohibited behaviors, folding the arms tightly across the chest is also another behavior that came in during threatening situations. As teenage checks in, kids will learn how to make the gesture of crossed arms more evident by relaxing the hands and arms just a little bit. They would also accompany the signals with legs that are crossed.

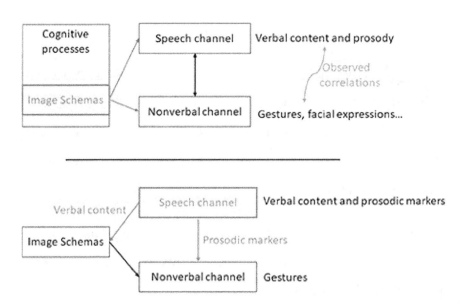

Defensive Arms Display

The gesture of folding the arm has been upgraded to the extent where now people try to make it even less evident to others who are seeing them. When a single or both the arms are folded, maybe across the chest, a barrier is then created.

This is one of the ways of blocking all that might be perceived as threats or situations that are undesirable. When arms are neatly folded across the regions of the lungs and heart, it is a sign of protecting these very vital organs. That shows that the behavior of crossing the arms could be inborn.

One thing that is for sure is that when a person has a defensive, or nervous attitude, there are possible chances that he will have his hands tightly on the chest as a sign of feeling threatened.

The Territorial Arm Displays

Status can also influence one to use a given arm folding gesture. A superior kind of person can make his superiority evident by failing to fold his hands, saying that they are not afraid of anything.

For instance, if a general manager of a firm is introduced in a company function, he will usually stand back from them, with his hands in his back or by his side or in a superiority position. At times, he can also put one of his hands in his pockets, which is a sign of non-involvement. In very rare cases will such a person fold his arms across the chest as an indication of the tinniest sign of being nervous.

Once they have shaken hands with the boss, the new employees might also opt to cross their aims either fully or partially because of their main apprehension of being in the company of the highest leader of the company.

Both the company's GM and the new workers will feel very comfortable with their respective gesture clusters as each one of them is signaling his status that is relative to the other.

However, things might get a different twist when the GM meets a young and upcoming male individual who might display some superiority and even signal that he is as important as the general manager.

What happens is that after the two have given everyone a dominant handshake, the upcoming young officials may be forced to fold their arms as a signal with both the thumbs folding in the upward direction.

The gesture shows two arms that are crossed and all the thumbs facing up, indicating that the individual is in control and feeling just okay. As he continues to speak, he will gesture with his thumbs as a means of displaying to others that he has a self-confident kind of attitude, and the arms that are folded still provided a sense of security.

A person who is not only feeling submissive and also very defensive will sit in symmetrically implying that the other part of their body is the best mirror to the other side. They will show the tone of a stressed muscle and appear like they are sensing an attack, while someone who is dominant and defensive will just opt to sit in an asymmetrical way, where one part of the body does not mirror the other.

How To Spot Insecurity In The Rich And Famous

People who are usually exposed to others, such as movie stars, TV personalities, politicians, and royalties usually don't intend their audience to realize that they either nervous or unsure of what they are doing or saying when they are on the limelight.

When on display, these people usually prefer to project a controlled, calm, and cool attitude each time they are on display.

However, their apprehension or anxiety normally comes out in not so good forms such as the crossing of arms. Like it is the case with all arm-crossing signals, a single arm swings across the body in the direction of the other arm, but instead of the arms getting to cross each other, one hand touches or hold on to a watch, or a handbag on or close to their other arm. For another time, the boundary is created, and the feeling of security is attained.

Men who wear cufflinks are usually captured fixing and adjusting them when they cross the dance floor or a room full of people. Adjusting the cuff-links was one of the trademarks of Prince Charles, who applied it to feel secure each moment he walked across an open place fully aware that there are other people who are watching them.

One would be deceived to believe that after close to a whole century of being confronted by large crowds and scrutinized in public, royals like Prince Charles will try to resist some of the nervous feelings that are revealed by his small arm-crossing.

A self-conscious and anxious man will usually find himself trying to adjust the band on his wristwatch, rubbing his hands together or checking what are contained in their wallets. At times, they can also be seen playing with the buttons on their cuff or even using any gestures that enable his arms to cross in front of their body.

One of the most favorite gestures for a businessman who is insecure is making in ways to an official event holding a folder or briefcase in front of their bodies. To someone who has some training, these signals are just giveaways since they achieve no definite aim as opposed to a try to hide their nervousness.

If there is a better place of observing these body signals, then it has to be at any place where individuals walk past a large group of bystanders. A good example would be a man who moves to the dancing podium to look for a female dancer who can join him on the dance floor or a person who cross the stage to go and get an award.

The use of hidden arm barriers by women is not easily noticeable as that of men. This is because women will be able to grasp into things such as purses or handbags if they are unsure of themselves or become self-conscious. Princess Anne and other loyalties would usually clutch some flowery items each time they are making inroads in public.

The flowers and handbag clutch are the favorite for Queen Elizabeth. There are very limited chances that she would be carrying lipstick, theatre tickets, and credit cards in the purse.

Instead of that, she applies this as a kind of safety blanket when necessary and as a way of sending out a strong message. The royal watchers have recorded a total of twelve signs that she sends to her minders whenever she wants to leave, go, or be taken from a conversation she does not enjoy.

There is a very usual means of creating a strong barrier is to carry up a glass of cup with two hands. Usually, one would only need one hand to hold the cup, but two hands will enable the insecure person to create a nearly invisible boundary. These kinds of signals are applied nearly by everyone, and there are some of us who are fully aware that we are applying them.

The Legs Reveal The Mind's Intentions

The more distant from the human brain a body part is placed, the less awareness the human being have of what is really happening with the body. Most people, for instance, are much aware of their face and the kind of signs and expressions that they are showing to the public. As a matter of fact, there are certain expressions that we can practice, such as putting on a brave face or looking unhappy when disappointed by a close friend or relative.

After our face, the body parts that we are much less aware of got to be our hands and arms. They are closely followed by our stomach and chest, and we are also not so much aware of our legs and nearly oblivious to our feet.

This implies that the legs and the feet are a very vital information source regarding the attitude of a person since most people are not so much aware of what they are doing with these body parts and do not think of faking gestures with them in the manner they might apply with their face.

Someone who is appearing composed and in full control while the foot is taping repeatedly or making short jabs in the air shows their frustrations at being unable to escape away from the trap they are.

How To Analyze The Nonverbal Signals Of The Legs

Several tests that were conducted with a couple of company managers sometime in the past made clear certain revelations. The managers had been asked to lie in a convincing manner in many staged interviews. Regardless of their genders, the managers increased the unconscious number of foot movements that they had made while lying.

A good number of these managers also applied unreal facial expressions and attempted to offer control to their hands while resting, but nearly all were not aware of what their legs and feet were doing.

According to the psychologist who verified the results, apart from increasing the movements of their lower bodies when people lie, observers have higher success when it comes to exposing the lies of a person each time they can see the whole body of the liar.

This explains why a few business moguls appear so comfortable and relaxed only when sitting behind a desk that has a very strong and concrete front.

This is because they can hide their lower bodies. Glass tables cause more stress as compared to the solid ones. This is because when the legs can be fully seen, and therefore, we might not feel as if we are entirely in control.

The human legs have evolved with time to serve two main aims; to run away from danger and to move forward to obtain food. Since the human brain has been hardwired for these two main purposes, how a person uses the feet and leg to show where they want to move.

To make it more understandable, they tend to show the commitment of a person to either stay or leave a conversation. The uncrossed or open leg positions shows a dominant attitude. On the other hand, the crossed leg positions reveal that an attitude that is uncertain or closed.

A woman who has no interest in a man might opt to fold her arms on the chest and cross the legs so much from him, which can be defined as a *no-go body language*. A woman who is interested, on the other hand, would willingly open herself to him.

Why Are The Legs Accurate Reflections Of Our Emotional State?

Even though they are usually neglected in the study of body language, our legs and feet tell a lot of vulnerable information that regard what we are thinking, sensing, and feeling. As noted earlier in the book, much attention is paid to the face and other body parts and entirely forgets about these two vital parts of the body.

As a matter of fact, both the legs and the feet are the most accurate parts of a human body. Apart from reflecting our true emotions, they also show the intentions that we have. They do all these in real time, unlike some parts of our bodies like the face.

They can also be very vital in detecting some of the lies that we tell. In the past years, the human limbic system has ensured that our legs and feet reacted instantly to any concern or threat, and their reliability has always assured us of our survival.

A child may be sitting down to have a meal, but you will notice how the feet sway when they want to go out and play. You will also be able to see this on the way they stretch to reach the floor from a high chair even at times when they haven't finished eating.

Yet an attempt could be made to ensure that the child remains seated, but he will continue wiggling, and his feet will then turn towards an exit that is nearby.

This is a perfect example of where he wants to go. This can be referred to as an intention cue, and there are quite a lot that can be used to show our needs for doing a given task. Since both the legs and the feet are very honest, a great emphasis is placed in what they communicate while assessing for any possible instance of deception. Many people prefer to focus on the face, which is so unfortunate since our faces perform the best when it comes to deceit.

Just as kids grow up, they will always be reminded not to "make that face," and grow with that habit into adulthood. Young adults will put up a party face at the mere request of their loved ones or just smile since the culture we were brought up in needs it that way.

For purposes of social harmony, people fake what they think or feel with their faces. It is also done as a way of protecting oneself from being discovered out when they are not so honest. Both the legs and the feet make no similar concessions since they are necessary for survival purposes.

Boredom, caution, anxiety, fear, stress, nervousness, anger, lethargy, depression, subservience, confidence, awkwardness, humility, coyness, shyness, hurt, joy, happiness, relentlessness can also manifest through the legs and feet. It has also been proved beyond reasonable doubt that people will often distance themselves from others when they begin to lie. They do this by standing further away from you or they even point their feet so far away from you, but occasionally make a turn towards you using their torso.

On the first inspection, this behavior might just look okay. However, the truth is that these are distancing behaviors that reveal quite much concerning what is going on in the human brain. Liars always try to focus on the lies they are telling but just forget to also focus on the emotions that accompany what they are saying.

These reveal certain behaviors that defy the gravity each time they open their mouths to speak.

Those who are truthful tend to challenge this kind of gravity by rising straight on their feet each time they are trying to emphasize on a certain topic. At times, they could also be seen trying to arch their eyebrows.

There is a reason why liars do not do that. This is because behaviors that defy gravity are derived limbic ally. These are the emotional exclamations that are expressed through the body language that they do not have.

Each time we are saying something that is true, the feet will usually take a sturdier and broader stance. Immediately we sense insecurity about what we are saying or if we are not honest in our submissions, the feet will come together for another time.

Again, it is very important to note that this is also a limbic response that is strongly tethered to the kind of feelings that we have concerning what is being said. This will be evident in our legs each time we are not mentally sure of what we are saying.

When saying something that is not so true, the deceiver will usually try to be more concerned about being detected, and the concerns might, at times, drive what is known as the Ankle Quiver.

In this case, the ankle will start to twitch, causing the individual to rock foot in a sideways direction. Someone who is telling the truth does not need that type of repetitive rocking habit, but a liar will usually find under the table behaviors such as those to be so soothing to them. There are several foot and leg behaviors that can be seen out there.

It is very important to look for someone who makes a statement and then does what can be referred to as a leg cleanse. By rubbing his hands on the top of his legs while they are seated, the person who is telling a liar will be appeased. It can also happen to a person who is hiding some guilty knowledge.

How To Analyze People Via The Nonverbal Of The Hands And Palm

For a long time, the hands have been used as one of the most vital tools in the evolution of human. There are many connections that exist between the brain and the hand than any other body part. There are just a handful of people who ever check how their hands appear and behave or how they shake their hands when they meet a new person.

Despite all that, the hands can be used to establish whether power plays, dominance, and submission will occur. All across the history of humanity, the open palm has usually been connected to honesty, truth, submission as well as allegiance.

How Hand Movements Boost Your Credibility And Persuasiveness

When individuals desire to be honest or open, they will usually hold either of their palms out to the other individual and utter words such as "I didn't do it," or "I'm telling the truth." When a person starts to be truthful or open in all that they are saying, they are likely to expose either part or all of their palms to the person they are speaking to.

Just as it is with some body signs, this is an entirely unconscious body sign that offers a hunch or intuitive that the other individual is saying the truth.

When kids are concealing something or trying to lie, they will usually hide their palms right behind their backs.

In the same manner, a man who desires to hide his whereabouts after spending some night out with his crew might also put his palms in his pockets, or even in an arm-crossed-kind of posture as he attempts to explain to his partner where he had been.

Salespersons are also trained to look out for the exposed palms of the customers when they offer objections or reasons about why they are unable to purchase a given product. This is because when a person is offering legit reasons, they will always display their palms.

When people opt to be truthful when it comes to explaining the reasons that they have, they will flash their palms and use their hands, while a person who is not saying the truth will offer the same verbal responses but tend to hide their hands.

Putting the hands in the pockets is one of the greatest ploys used by men who do not wish to indulge in any kind of conversation. Initially, the palms were designed to be the body's vocal cords.

This is because they usually talk mush as compared to any other part of the body and placing them away appeared like keeping a person numb all the time.

Analyzing People Through their Handshakes

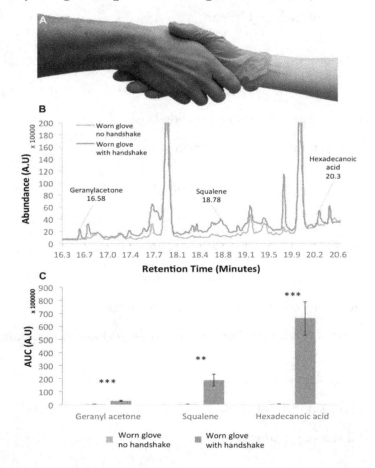

Handshake is one of the relics of our old past. Each time the traditional and so cultural tribes met under some conducive conditions, they'd usually hold their arms out with the palms shown out as a sign of that no weapon was either being concealed or hidden.

During Roman times, carrying a hidden weapon like a dagger in the sleeve was one of the safety mechanisms. As a result, the

Romans went ahead and developed a common greeting that was known as Lower-Arm-Grasp.

Interlocking and shaking of the palms is the modern form of this type of traditional greeting. This method was used in the nineteenth century as a way of sealing business operations between men who were in the same economic class.

Japan is one of the places where the traditional greeting was bowing, and Thailand where the word Wai is used when greeting each other, but the modern handshake is now getting to be used in those places. In many areas, the hands are usually pumped 5-7 times, while in other countries, the hands are pumped 2-3 times with an extra hold time that is equal to an additional two pumps.

One of the biggest glad-handers across the globe has to be French. They shake on both departure and greeting, and still spend a huge time still shaking hands.

Based on what has been said about the effects of Palm-Down and Palm-Up gestures, it is very important to investigate their main relevance when it comes to handshakes. During the times of the Romans, two main leaders would usually come together and greet one another with what would be referred to as a standing version of a modern-day arm wrestling.

If one of the two leaders were much stronger compared to the other, then his hand would complete right above the hand of the other person in the infamous Upper Hand position — assuming that you have just come across a person for the very first time and you initiate handshake when greeting them.

One of the three main attitudes will be transmitted in a subconscious manner:

1   Dominance – "The person is trying to dominate me, and so it would be very important for me to be very cautious."

2   Submission – "I can be able to dominate this kind of person. He will do all that I desire and ask him."

3   Equality – "I feel very comfortable with this kind of person."

Some of these attitudes are received and sent without us being so much aware of all these enlisted. However, they can have an immediate effect on the outcome of the meeting. Turning a hand so that the palms can face down in the handshake usually transmits dominance. The palms shouldn't directly face down.

A study was undertaken for a group of top management officers. In that study, it became evident that apart from nearly all the managers initiating the handshake, 31% of the females and 88% of the males applied the dominant handshake position. Issues that pertain to control and power are usually less important to the women, which could be the main reason why one in a group of three women tried out the Upper Hand Ritual.

It has also been observed that there are certain groups of men that will usually offer the male a soft handshake in certain social contexts as a way of showing submissiveness. This is one of the best ways of implying that dominating a woman could be so easy or even highlighting their femininity.

However, in a business context, this approach can be very dangerous to a woman since the male will decide to offer attention to the feminine features and will rarely take her seriously. Females who show high femininity in business events are rarely taken seriously by a few other businessmen and women, even though it is now politically or fashionably correct to say that everyone is the same.

This does not imply that a businesswoman wants to appear to be masculine; she needs to avoid signs of the woman-ness such as short skirts, handshakes, and high heels if she needs equal credibility. The submissive handshake is also another kind of handshake that is commonly used.

There is a defined opposite of this engaging handshake. It is to offer one's hands with the palms facing up, symbolically offering the other person the upper hand, such as a dog that is exposing its throat to another dog that is more superior. This can be very effective when you want to offer the other person control or allow him to feel that he is fully in charge of the situation at hand, for instance, if you were offering an apology.

The gesture clusters that they use as a result of their handshake will offer you further clues for the assessment of them. On the other hand, someone who is very submissive will use several submissive gestures, whereas someone who is dominant will use assertive gestures to pass a message.

When two dominant individuals opt to use the handshake, a special kind of power struggle occurs as every individual tries to turn the other person's palms into the submissive position.

The outcome of this is a kind of handshake with all the palms left out in the main vertical area, and this would create a feeling of mutual respect and equality since none of them is ready to give in to the other person.

There are also two main items for coming up with a rapport in the whole issue of a handshake. Firstly, it is important to ensure that the palms of the other person are in a vertical position so that none of them is submissive or dominant.

The same pressure should be applied. This implies that if, on a firmness scale of one to ten, the handshake will record a seven while the other individual will only record a 5. It will be very important to back off 20% in total strength. This is to say that if their grip is nine and yours is seven, then it would be very important to grow the grip by 20%.

If you were to meet less than 20 people, maybe just 10, it would be very important to make some improvements of intensity and angle to come up with a rapport with all the people and to stay on a same footing with each of the individuals.

It is also very important to remember that the average male hand can exert about twice as the average power a female hand can, and therefore, there should be allowances for this precise need. With the evolution of man, male hands can now exert a whole grip of up to hundred pounds, which translates to about 45 kilograms, for the actions such as carrying, gripping, tearing, hammering and even throwing.

It is also very important to remember that the whole issue of handshake evolved with time as a sign to mean goodbye or hello or even seal a strong agreement, so it often needs to be positive, and warm.

The palm-down thrust can just be compared to one of the most popular salutation styles that were used by the Nazi. It is one of the most aggressive types of handshake since it offers the receiver just a small chance to create up an equal relationship.

This kind of handshake is typical of the dominant and overbearing person who usually starts it, and their arm with the palm facing the downward position forces the receiver to be in a submissive position. If you think that a person is offering a palm-down thrust to you on purpose, there are a number of counters to it;

The step-to-the-right methodology - If you have been offered a so indulging handshake from a power player kind-of-person, it is not just hard to turn the palm upwards in a position that is equal, but it will also be just easy and simple when you do it.

This methodology includes moving forward using the left foot as you make the step to shake the hands. This will need some sort of practice since stepping forward on the right foot is just a normal position for close to 90% of people when they are shaking with their right hand.

The next step is to make a forward move (step) with your right leg, moving across in front of the person and also out of his personal space. The last step would be to bring the left leg over to the right one to finish up the process of maneuver and shake the person's hands.

This tactic enables one to make a straight handshake or even opt to turn it over to the submissive kind of position. It basically feels as if a person is walking across in front of another person and can just be compared to winning an arm-wrestling with another person.

This also makes it so easy to take full control by invading the personal space of the other person. It is very important to analyze the main approach of shaking hands and take note of the foot that you step forward using, particularly when you extend your arm to give a handshake.

There are people who use the right foot and so are at a disadvantage when they need to do a handshake since they have very little room to make movements and it enables the other person to dominate.

It is also very important to step into a handshake with the left foot, and you will notice that it is so easy to deal with the power players who might want to take full control of the whole situation.

There is also the hand-on-top technique that is so popular. When a power player type of a person opts to present to you a palm-down thrust, it is very important to respond using your main hand while the palm is raised up before placing the left hand over his right hand to create what is known as a double-hander, and then ensure that the handshake is straight.

This action will seek to switch the power from the power player to you and is also one of the easiest ways of taking full control of the situation. It is also one of the easiest handshake styles that women can use.

If you have a feeling that a power player is purposefully making attempts of intimidating you, and he does it so regularly, then the best thing is to get hold of his hand on top and then shake it. It is an action that will shock the power player, and therefore, it is important to be selective when using this handshake. It should be the last resort.

Nobody would rejoice in a handshake that makes it feel as if you have been handed some cold beverage sausages. Each time we become tensed when in company of strangers, the blood will divert far from the cells below the skin's outer layer on the hands, that is usually called the dermis.

It will then move to the leg and arm muscles for the fight and flight preparation. The outcome is that the hands will lose some temperature and start to produce some sweat.

The double-hander is also another favorite type of handshake. It is usually delivered with a direct eye-to-eye contact. The other thing that accompanies this type of handshake is an assuring smile as well as confidently repeated mention of the first name of the receiver.

After all that, a serious inquiry of the current state of health of the receiver usually follows. This type of handshake tends to increase the physical contact usually offered by the initiator and in addition tends to offer some dominion over the main receiver by basically stopping his right hands.

At times known as the politician's handshake, the initiator of this kind of handshake will try to offer an impression and assurance that he is honest and trustworthy.

However, when it is used on two people that have just met, it can tend to have certain reverse effects and leave the receiver in a situation that they feel suspicious regarding the main intentions of the initiator.

The double hander can just be compared to a kind of hug and is only applied in situations where a hug could also be allowed. 90% of human beings can throw away the right arm in front of the whole body, in a process that is known as an over-arm blow. This is usually done for primary self-defense.

To restrict this type of defense capability, the double hander must be used, which explains the reason why it should never be applied in salutations where there is no personal bond that exists between you and other people.

It should also be used in situations where an emotional bond is already in existence, like in the case of meeting a longtime ally. In all these situations, self-protection is not a very vital issue, and so the handshake could be very genuine.

Chapter 2:

Analyzing People through the Nonverbals of the Face

The face is used more often than any other part of the body for covering up dishonesty. We usually use nods, winks and smiles in our bids to cover up some of the lies that we tell.

However, as unfortunate as it might seem, our main gestures will always show the truth since there is an absence of harmony between our facial signs and body signals.

Our emotions and attitudes are revealed on our faces, something that we are almost not aware of all the times.

Each time that we try to conceal and lie, or an inevitable thought pops out in our minds; it can be displayed for just some minutes on our faces.

In most cases, a person's fast nose touch has been interpreted as a mere itch, or people are deeply interested in us when they rest their hands on their faces.

A man was once recorded on film on how he coexisted well with his mother-in-law. But every time the man called the name of his mother-in-law, his face's left side raised in a manner just took about a split second. Contrary to what could be seen, the man still went ahead to say how he really felt, which contradicted the writings on his face.

Nonverbal Gestures Of The Eye

Across history, we have been taken much with the eyes and the effect that they have on human behavior. Eye to eye contact tends to regulate the conversation and then provides cues of dominance.

Much of our times are spent staring at the face of the other person. Therefore, eye gestures are one of the most important parts of being able to read the thoughts and attitudes of a person. Each time people get in touch for the very first time, they tend to commit several quick judgments about each other, entirely depending on what they can see.

Common says and phrases like "he appeared daggers at her" or maybe an expression such as "she has shifty eyes." It is also said that a person has bedroom eyes, Spanish eyes, Bette Davis eyes, or maybe piercing eyes.

When these phrases are used, we tend to refer to the size of the pupils of the individual and his stare behavior. The eyes can be very accurate and showing of all the communication signals that the human has. This is because the signals are the body's main balancing point, and the pupils also operate in an independent way to control their own conscious.

The Dilating Pupils

In conditions where there is full light, the pupils will either contract or dilate as there is a change in the mood and attitude from positive to negative and the vice versa.

When a person gets happy, their pupils will dilate to up to 4 sizes their ordinary and normal size. On the other hand, a negative or angry mood will make the pupils reduce in size to what is usually known as snake eyes or beady little eyes.

Eyes that are lighter can appear more attractive since they are so easy to notice the dilation that is occurring. According to the former head of the Department of Psychology at the University of Chicago, Eckhard Hess, the size of the pupil will be affected by the general condition of the arousal of a person.

Eckhard is also among the first people who introduced the studies of pupillometry. In general, the size of the pupil will increase when people view something that tends to stimulate them.

According to Hess, the pupils of women who are all heterosexuals and men will dilate when seeing the pin-ups of the opposite sex and tend to constrict when viewing the same-sex pin-ups.

Studies that are similar have also been obtained when a group of people was told to look at unpleasant and pleasant pictures that included politicians, foods, war scenes, or children who are disabled. The feeling can also be repeated when listening to a certain type of music.

Hess also discovered that the increase in the size of the eye pupil is correlated positively with a mental activity that relates to solving certain problems, hitting the maximum dilation when a person gets to the solution.

When this study is applied in the business markets, it will demonstrate how the models are rated in photos appear very beautiful when the image has been modified to make the pupil section to look larger.

It was one of the best ways of maximizing marketing and sales of any type of product that apply the close up of a face, like the cosmetics of women, the clothing and hair products.

The eyes are one of the major signals in courtship, and the main aim of the eye make-up is to make an emphasis on the display of the eye. If for instance, a woman has some attractions to a male counterpart, she will go ahead to dilate the pupils as she looks into his eyes, and the man is likely to decipher this signal in the best way without even realizing it.

This explains why many romantic instances are very successful in places that aren't properly lit. It is because the pupils of the eyes will dilate and tend to show that the couples are just having some interest in each other.

When those who are in love stare deep into the eyes of each other, they are looking for the signals of pupil dilation unknowingly, and each one of them will become excited by the dilation of the pupils of the others.

Another study has also shown that when men watch pornographic films, their pupils will dilate to nearly three times their size. Most pupils that belong to women offered the highest dilation when they were checking out the images of mothers and (their) babies.

Children and toddlers tend to have larger pupils as compared to the adults, and pupils belong to the babies will dilate at constant times when the adults are present and, in an attempt, to appear so much appealing to the adults.

As a result, they then get constant and quick attention. This also explains why the top-selling children toys have always been designed with oversized pupils.

A study has also proved it that the dilation of a pupil has a given some influence on the person who views the dilated pupils. Men who check pictures of women who have dilated pupils showed that they had greater dilation of the pupil than when views pictures of women that had constrained pupils.

The pupils of the men predictably dilated highly when they saw the pictures of the women without clothes on, while gay men dilated most at the men who were without clothes.

However, the pupils of the women dilated most at the picture of the mother and the baby with the naked male picture acquiring the second position.

Tests that are carried with professional card players show that professionals won a smaller number of games when their opponents were in dark glasses.

For instance, if an opponent was dealt 4 aces in an amazing game such as that of poker, the rapid dilation of the pupil could be detected by the professional, who would occasionally sense that he should not bet on the next hand.

The dark glasses that were put on by the opponents got rid of all the pupil signals, and the outcome is that the professionals got in lesser hands than the normal ones. Decoding of the pupils was also used in the old-time gem traders from China who watched for the dilation of the pupil of their buyers when they were negotiating for the products' prices.

Some few centuries ago, commercial sex workers or prostitutes placed some few drops of belladonna, which was a tincture that contained a chemical called atropine, into the eyes so that they can dilate their pupils and make themselves look so desirable.

According to a famous old cliché, it was said that it is important to look a person in the eye when having a conversation with them or even when having a negotiation with them. However, it is much better to look them in the pupil since it is only the pupil that will tell the whole truth. It is also very important to note that human beings are the only primates that have sclera, which is the white side of the eye. The eyes of the apes, on the other hand, have completely dark eyes.

The white of the eyes have been able to evolve with time from the time it was used an aid for communication to enable people to know where the other people were all looking since the vector is usually directed to the emotional stress. The female brains are much hardwired when compared to that of their male counterparts. The brain of the men is more designed to be able to comprehend the emotions, and one of the consequences of this is that the women have whiter when compared to the men. As noted previously, the eyes of the apes lack the eye-whites, which implies that their prey does not know where the ape is exactly looking or even whether they have been spotted. This, in return, gives the ape a higher chance of getting for more hunting chances.

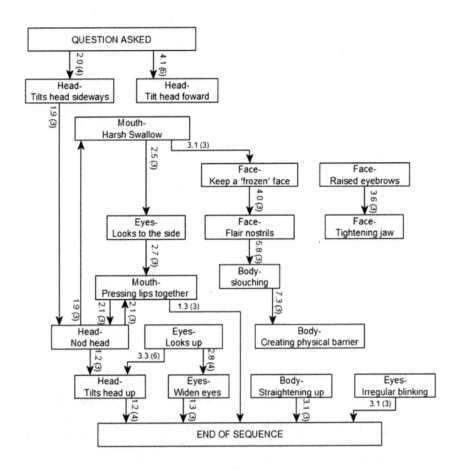

Chapter 3:

Ways of Telling If Someone is Lying

act is that only 54% of the lies can be spotted in an accurate manner. Research has also proved that extroverts tell more lies when compared to the introverts and not less than 82% of the lies usually go without being detected.

The big question here is how to detect that someone is lying. One of the initial steps in this whole process is getting with how someone typically acts, especially when they are speaking.

TRUNCATED AXIS

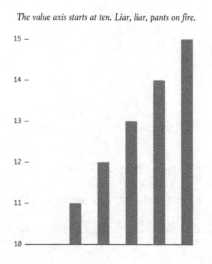

The value axis starts at ten. Liar, liar, pants on fire.

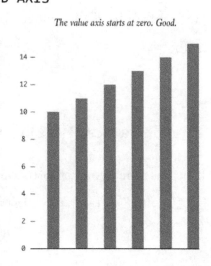

The value axis starts at zero. Good.

Basically, this is the process of coming up with known as a baseline. A baseline is essentially how a person acts when they are under non-threatening and just normal conditions.

According to the Science of People website, it is basically how a person appears when they are saying the truth. To make it clearer, it might be a bit difficult to tell when a person is not speaking the fact if you are not sure of how they usually act when saying the truth, which, to a wider extent, makes a lot of sense.

However, the techniques that are used to determine if someone is lying can be very confusing. As a matter of fact, these strategies can even be very conflicting. Due to that, it is important to think twice before making an accusation, ensure that you feel more than once about doing it unless it is important to go ahead and find out what happened.

Here are some of the telltale signs that someone is not telling the truth;

The Behavioral Delay Or Pause

It begins when you ask someone a question, and you get no reply initially. The person then begins to respond after some delay. There is one big question that should be asked here; how long should the delay extend before it becomes meaningful before it can be regarded as a deceptive sign? It, however, depends on a few factors.

You can try this particular exercise on a friend, and ask a question like this, "What were you doing on a day like this six years ago.

After asking that question, you will notice that the person will take an invariable pause before answering the question. This is because it is not a type of question that naturally evokes a fast and immediate answer.

Even as the person takes time to think about the question, he might still not be able to give a meaningful response. The next question to ask would be this," Did you rob a cloth shop on this day six years ago?" if they make a pause before giving you the answer you need, then it would be very important to pick the kind of friends you have wisely.

In most cases, there will be no pause, and the person is likely to respond by just saying no and letting the story die.

This is a simple test that tends to drive home the point that the delays should usually be considered out of the church of God. in the context of whether; it is appropriate for the question at hand.

The Verbal or non-verbal disconnect

The human brains have been wired in a manner that causes both the nonverbal and the verbal behaviors to match up in a natural manner. So, each time, there is a disconnect, it is usually regarded as a very important deceptive indicator. A very common verbal or nonverbal disconnect that you should look out for will occur when someone nods affirmatively while giving a "No" answer. It might also occur when a person moves his head from one end to the other when giving a "Yes" answer.

If you were to carry out that mismatch, as an example, to offer a response to a question, then you will realize that you will have to force yourself through the motion that you have. But despite all that, someone who is deceptive will still do it without even giving it a second thought.

There are a number of caveats that have been connected to this type of indicator. First of all, this type of indicator is not applicable in a short phrase or one-word response. Instead, it is only suitable in a narrative response. For instance, consider that a human head might make a quick nodding motion when a person says "No." That is just a simple emphasis and not a disconnect.

Second, it is also very important not to forget that a nodding motion does not necessarily mean "Yes' in certain cultures. In such cultures, a side-to-side head motion also does not imply that the person is saying "No."

Hiding The Eyes Or The Mouth

Deceptive people will always hide their eyes or mouth when they are not saying the truth. There is a tendency to desire to cover over a given lie, so if the hand of a person moves in front of their mouth while they are making a response to a given question, which becomes significant.

In a similar instance, hiding the eyes can be an inclination to shield a person from the outlash of those they could be lying to. If an individual shield or covers their eyes when they are responding to a question, what they could also be showing, on the level of subconscious, is that they can't bear to see the reaction to the lie they are saying.

In most cases, this kind of eye shielding could be done using the hand, or the person could as well decide to close the eyes. Blinking is not in the picture here, but when a person closes their eyes while making a response to a question that doesn't need reflection to answer, which can be considered as a way of hiding the eyes, hence becoming a possible deceptive indicator.

Swallowing or Throat Clearing

If a person loudly swallows saliva or clears the throat before answering a given question, then there is a problem somewhere. However, if any of these actions are performed after they have answered the question, then there is nothing to worry about. But when it happens before answering a question, then there are some things that should be analyzed. The person could be doing the nonverbal equivalent of the following verbal statements," I swear to God…"'This is one of the ways of dressing the lie in the best attires before presenting it. Looking at it from the physiological point of view, the question might have created a type of anxiety spike, which can as well as cause dryness and discomfort in the throat and mouth.

The Hand-to-Face Actions

The other way of determining if someone is saying a lie is to check what they do with their faces or in the head region each time they are asked a question. Usually, this would take the form of licking or biting the lips or even pulling the ears or lips together. The main reason behind this reflects one of the simple science questions that are usually discussed in high school. When you have someone a question, and you notice that it creates a kind of spike in anxiety, what you should remember is that the right response will be damaging. In return, that will activate the autonomic nervous system to get to business and try to dissipate the anxiety, which might appear to drain a lot of blood from the surface of the extremities, ears, and the face.

The effects of this could be a sensation of itchiness or cold. Without the person even realizing it, his hands will be drawn to the mentioned areas, and there could be rubbing or wringing of the hands. And just like that, you might have spotted a deceptive indicator.

The Nose Touch

Women usually carry out this special gesture with smaller strokes compared to those of men, as a way of avoiding smudging of their make-ups. One of the most important things to recall is that this kind of action should be read in context and clusters, as the person could have any hay of cold or fever.

According to a group of scientists at the Smell & Taste Treatment and Research Foundation that is based in Chicago, when someone lies, chemicals that are called catecholamine are released and make the tissue that is inside the nose to swell.

The scientists applied a special imaging camera that reveals the blood flow in the body and show that deliberate lying can also lead to an increase in the blood pressure. This technology proves that the human nose tends to expand with blood when someone lies, and that is what is referred to as the Pinocchio Effect.

Maximized blood pressure will also inflate the nose and make the nervous nose tingle, leading to a kind of brisk rubbing with the hand to suppress the itching effect.

The swelling cannot be seen with the naked eyes, but it is usually what causes the nose touch gesture. The same phenomenon will also take place when a person is angry, anxious, and upset. American psychiatrist Charles Wolf and neurologist Alan Hirsch carried out a detailed analysis of the testimony of Bill Clinton to the Grand Jury on the affair he had with Monica Lewinsky.

They realized that each time he was being honest, he rarely touched his nose. However, when he lied, he offered he appeared to be wearing a frown before he gave the answer and touched his nose once each 4 minutes for a mega total of 26 nose touches.

The scientists also said the former US president didn't touch his nose at all when he offered the answers to the questions in a truthful manner.

Eye Rub

When a child does not want to see something, the only thing they will do is to cover their eyes. They usually do this with both of their hands. On the other hand, when an adult does not want to see something distasteful to them, they are likely to rub their eyes. The eye is one of the attempts by the brain to block out a doubt, deceit, or any distasteful thing that it sees.

It is also done to avoid looking at the face of the person who the lie is being said to. Usually, men would firmly rub their eyes, and they may look away if the myth is a real whopper.

Women are not so likely to use the eye rub gesture. Instead, they will use gentle and small touching emotions just beneath the eyes since they either want to avoid interfering with the makeups they are wearing, or they have been redesigned as girls to stay away from making several gestures. At times, they might also want to avoid the listener's gaze by trying to look away.

One of the commonly used phrases out there is lying through the teeth. It is used to refer to a cluster of gestures portraying fake smile and clenched teeth, accompanied by the famous eye rub. It is a common gesture that is used by movie actors to show some level of dishonesty and by other traditions such as English, who will prefer not to say what they are exactly thinking.

The Neck Scratch Gesture

The index finger will usually scratch the side of the neck that is below the area of the earlobe. The reservations that have been made out of this gesture is that a person will rub their neck at an average five times. There are sporadic cases where the number of scratches is usually less than five.

Similarly, there is hardly any instance where the number of times a person scratches his neck exceeds five. This gesture can be used as a sign of doubt and can be used to characterize the person who says, "I am not so sure." It is so easy to notice when there is a contradiction between the verbal language and the gesture itself. For instance, when a person says words such as, "I can understand what you are undergoing," the neck sign should be checked as it could be indicating something different.

The collar pull is also another strong gesture that is normally used. Desmond Morris was the first person that made a discovery that telling lies cause a sort of tingling sensation in the tissues of the neck or the delicate facial. The only remedy for this was either a scratch or a rub.

Apart from proving why uncertain people will always scratch their neck, it also gives a better reason as to why some individuals use the collar pull when they lie and think that they might have been caught. Maximized blood pressure from the person telling a lie will make the person sweaty in the neck regions, especially when they feel that their untruthfulness has been discovered out.

It also happens when someone is either feeling frustrated or angry and wants to pull the collar away from his neck as a way of letting the cool air to circulate.

When a person is seen using this gesture, this is the question that they should be asked, "Could you kindly repeat that?" When the would-be deceiver is asked a question of that sort, they might be forced to give the game away.

Finger in the Mouth Gesture

This is one of the most unconscious ways of a person to revert to the security of a kid who is sucking on the breast of his/her mother and usually happens when an individual is under some pressure.

A toddler or a way much younger will usually substitute his/her thumb or even a cloth for the breast of her mother, and as they grow to become adults, they will put their fingers to their mouths and even suck on glasses, chews gum, pipes of pens and other things.

A few hands to mouth signals can be easily associated with lying or even deception, although the fingers in the mouth is an outward sign of an internal need of reassurance. Therefore, offering the individual assurances and guarantees is one of the best and positive moves they can be given.

Chapter 4:

Analyzing People in Dating and Love

L ove entails just several things; giggles and butterflies, comfort and happiness, best friendships and commitments. But love, contrary to what people think, is not easy to get. The modern day-to-day world offers two new ways of finding love – speed dating and online matchmaking.

In the last couple of years, the two main methods have moved from the final resort for the loveless to a more fully accepted means of the millions across the world to try and get their love mates.

Whereas this has led to relationships, dates and a couple of marriages across the world, it has also been a great boon for the enterprising researchers – offering a high number of datasets that are trying to chronicle the real-world behavior.

A huge number of psychological experts have also been involved in the study of love, attraction, as well as romantic relationships for the longest time possible. However, both speed dating and online matching have provided the researchers with an unprecedented chance to explore who is attracted to whom and the main reason behind all this.

Human beings, for millions of years, have been picking their love mates using the information that is usually gleaned in their face-to-face interactions. They, however, do not look at the appearance, but certain features such as the body language, the tone of the voice, body scent and not forgetting the immediate feedback that they get to their communications. The following questions also came up:

- Does the selection of mates differ when the people looking are given nearly the overwhelming number of potential partners, but are limited to a few statistics, photos, as well as an introductory paragraph about each one of them?
- What kind of information mostly captures the attention of the online daters?
- Apart from the photos, are the words also key to a person's heart?

In given research that was undertaken by Australian online daters, 85% of them said that they would not get in touch with someone in the absence of a posted photo. This proved that physical appearance is, indeed, very important.

Another study that was carried out in 2008 and in which those who took part rated online profiles of real people confirmed that a high number of people would be willing to contact only people they have seen their posted photos.

However, the study dwelled on the criteria that made a number of the photos appear so attractive.

It was also vital to note that these descriptors of the fixed choice enabled the users to triage by easily getting rid of those who unable to meet their deal breaker process for a partner.

Those who carried out the study fully believed that the users of these online platforms make up for the lack of enough information that has been witnessed in various online profiles. This is usually done by filling in the blanks with the guesses that are based on tiny pieces of information.

Some studies have also theorized that those who use online dating sites could be wearing rose-colored glasses each time they are looking at the potential dates – they end up filling the information gaps with positive attributed in a potential love partner — in a single study, knowing more information that regards to a potential date resulted in high chances of liking them.

This is because it tends to touch out on the inconsistencies as well as the lowered opportunities to fill in the blanks that have positive inferences. With one partner who is particularly compatible, more information led to increased chances of liking.

When it comes to the online daters, it implies that an entirely detailed profile might end up attracting few, but a high number of compatible suitors.

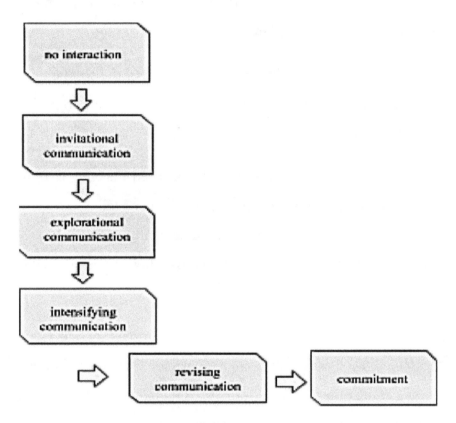

The study has also shown gender differences in both messaging and preference behavior on various online dating sites.

Men and women make a difference in the relative importance that they assign to different attributes of the potential partners.

Based on a study that was carried out by scientists drawn from Duke University, and the University of Chicago, an existing revolutionary theory discovered that in a sample of 22,000 online daters, females match income more than the physical attributes that include body mass index, height, facial attractiveness, when deciding on whom to contact.

Something of more importance is that these differences persist even when the issue of reproduction is out of the question. In one research that looked at those who are dating online across the lifespan, older men sought physical attractiveness and provided status-related information as compared to the women. Women, on the other hand, continued to be the more selective gender.

A study has also shown that even though the adage of "opposite sex attracts" appear to be true, it might turn out to be a false note. People are more likely to seek out a mate that is so like ourselves and then grow even more like each other, as the relationship gets stronger.

This is an idea that is supported by online dating research. A study carried out in 2005 by Fiore and Judith Donath from Massachusetts Institute of Technology monitored messaging data from more than 60,000 users of a dating site that was based in the United States. They found out that the users preferred sameness on all the categories that they tested.

However, there are a host of other factors that played more

important and larger roles than the others. The statuses that showed strongest same-seeking include married, having a kid, and wanting to have a kid. Fiore has also discovered that women responded more frequently than men who had the same popularity on the site.

According to Hitsch and the team he was working with, the similarity was highly preferred in several factors that included height, education, age, smoking, political views, and religion. They also discovered a very strong same-race preference.

Something that turned out to be interesting was that women had more pronounced same-race preferences, which is not usually revealed in their stated preferences. Even though the race preferences of the males appeared to be coinciding with their stated preferences, women also didn't want to admit to, or maybe were not even consciously aware of all these preferences.

According to a study that was carried out in 2014 revealed that men who were in a speed dating exercise needed their dates more when she played hard to get by appearing not to be interested in the questions that the men asked.

However, this kind of findings only applies in some given circumstances. Notably, the men had to feel as if they had a great affection to the woman, which, according to this research implied that they had picked her as their partner as opposed to being assigned to her.

It is also very important to note that, even though men needed the woman more when she played hard to get, the truth is that they wanted her less.

Displaying the Right Facial Expressions

Generally, happiness is very attractive to women and does not appear any attractive to men. In 2011, a group of researchers carried out a series of experiments on over 1000 people.

These people were shown photos of the members of the opposite sex and were then asked how the people were attractive on a given scale. According to the results that were obtained, men rated the women much more beautiful when they appeared happy and less attractive each time they tried to show some level of pride.

Women, on their side, rated the men most attractive each time they showed some signs of pride and least attractive when they appeared happy. Of interest is that shame was much attractive on both the women and men.

Nearly everybody has a given "type," even though women are likely to adhere to it as compared to their counterparts, men. In another study that was conducted in 2011, researchers were able to discover that both women and men rated opposite sex-faces much more attractive when they closely resembled their most recent or current partners.

However, men were less attracted to the faces that appeared like their current partner than how the women were.

A lot of hand gestures can also be used to analyze those who are in love. When you are looking for love, you should just put yourself out there. In other words, you should fill up the physical space that is around you with a high posture and hand gestures.

In another study that was carried out in 2016, researchers discovered that women and men in speed-dating sessions were twice as likely to say that they desired to see their partners again when the partners moved their arms and hands. It was different from when the partners sat in a still position.

The sentiments are supported by Glan Gonzaga, who is the main author of research of couples who got together on eHarmony. It also might make it so easy for the partners to comprehend each other in a better way. According to Gonzaga, this character trait could make it easier for partners to understand each other much better.

Staring into each other eyes for two minutes also have certain effects. Joan Kellerman, a psychologist at the University of Massachusetts, asked 72 unacquainted undergraduates to pair off and stare into each other's eyes for two minutes.

The undergraduates later reported that they had increased feelings of affection and passionate love towards the other person. According to a report by Scientific American, this suggests that extended periods of eye contact can be able to connect two people and go as far as igniting the feelings of love inside them.

It can even happen to two people who have never met.

Starting a relationship and making it glow appear to be based on how people attend to one another. With fourty-plus years of experience of studying couples, John Gottman, who is a psychologist, alludes that it is just a matter of bids.

For instance, if a wife who is fascinated with birds points out to her dear husband that a bird known as a goldfinch has just flown and landed in a tree that is nearby, the husband can turn away from her by dismissing the remark or even turn towards her by sharing the enthusiasm.

The results of such bids will always be staggering in, and in one of the studied of marriage that Gottman worked on, couples who dissolved their marriages after being together for 6 years had 33% as the turn-around reply of the time. On the other hand, couples that were still hooked upheld a turn around reply of 87% of the time.

Smelling in a certain way can also earn you a lover. Yes, that is according to a study undertaken sometime in the past at the University of California. The study was carried on women who were ovulating, and it suggested that some women preferred the smell of shirts or t-shirts put on by men with high levels of testosterone.

This study came into harmony with several hormone-based instincts. It went ahead to discover that there are a group of women that also have a strong liking for men with a very strong jawline during their ovulation period.

There are also some people that get attracted to individuals with the same eye or hair color of their opposite-sex parents. They also got attracted to people who had the same age range they witnessed tat birth.

This is according to a study that was carried out by David Perrett, who is a pathologist at the University of St. Andrew. According to Perrett, young ones less impressed women who were born to old parents, of more than 30 years.

When Two Opposite Sexes Meet: What Happens?

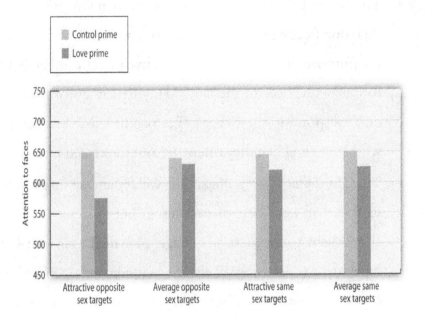

Just as it is with the animals, courtship of human beings also follows a certain predictable 5-step process. This is the circle that we all pass through each time we meet someone beautiful;

- The First Stage – The eye contact – A woman will look across the entire room and spot the man she adores a lot. She will wait until he notices her before holding his stare for close to five seconds before turning away. He will now keep on watching her see if that happens again. On average, a woman will need to bring this stare 3 times before the average man realize what could be going on. The stare procedure can be repeated several times, and it marks the beginning of the flirt process.

- The Second Stage – Smiling – The woman will give more than one fleeting smiles. This is a fast half smile that serves the purpose of offering the prospective man the green light to make advances to the lady. Many males, unfortunately, don't respond to these types of signs, therefore leaving the woman feeling like they (men) are not interested in them.

- The Third Stage – Preening – She will try and sit up straight to focus on her chest or even cross her ankles or legs to show them to the best advantage. She might also tilt her hips to one direction if she is standing, or even try to expose her bare neck. She might play with the hair for some time as an indication that she is letting herself groomed for the man. She might also flick her hair, lick her lips, and even straighten her jewelry and clothing. The man, on the other hand, might respond by rising straight, pulling his stomach in, adjusting his clothing, expanding his chest, or even touching his hair and tucking his thumbs into his belt. All these gestures will point either their whole bodies or feet towards each other.

- The Fourth Stage – Talk – The man will then approach and try to make small talk, sometimes using typical clichés such as "Haven't we met somewhere before?" They can also use some other fairly worn pick up lines, which are just supposed to break the ice and make the woman fall in.

- The Fifth Stage – Touch – The woman will look for a chance to initiate a very smooth touch on the arm; at times, it could be accidental or just intended. A touch in hand can be used to show a high degree of intimacy as compared to an arm touch. Each degree of the touch will be repeated to see if the person is enjoying that kind of intimacy. It is also done just to make them aware that the first touch was not accidental in any way.

Manipulation Tips And Tricks

Chapter 5:

Analyzing People via their Verbal Statements

E verything that a person does or says reveals something about their personality. Actions, beliefs, and thoughts of people are aligned perfectly with each other in a way that they all reveal the same things concerning an individual.

Just as it is said that all methods can lead to Rome, everything a person thinks or does can reveal a lot about their personality makeup and personality. The words that are spoken by a person, even if they appear to carry less weight, tell a great deal about a person's insecurities and desires.

No one doubts that the words we speak or write are a full expression of our inner personalities and thoughts. However, beyond the real content of a language, exclusive insights into the minds of the author are usually hidden in the text's style.

From our acts of dominance to truthfulness, we are revealing to others too much about us. You can quickly know the most important of all the people in the room by listening to the words that they use. Confident and high-status people use very few "I" words. The higher a person's status is in a given situation, the less the "I" words they will use in their conversations.

Each time people feel confident, they tend to focus on the task that they have at hand, and not necessarily on them. "I" is also used less in the weeks that follow a given cultural upheaval.

As age kicks on, we tend to use more positive emotional words and even make very fewer references to ourselves. A study has also shown it that the higher social class a person is, the fewer emotional words he will need to use.

According to Pennebaker, style words include auxiliary verbs, prepositions, pronouns, articles, and conjunctions. He also goes ahead to explain the content words, which include regular verbs, nouns, and especially adverbs and adjectives.

Here is the main difference between the style words and the content words. The content words are what someone is saying while the style words are how the words are said.

Women tend to use pronouns, social words, negations, as well as references to the psychological processes as compared to the male.

This could be a surprise, but men tend to use more big numbers, prepositions, and articles than women. But despite all that, the way women speak implies that human beings are more open and self-aware to the self-reflection. That is, according to Pennebaker, who also discovered that there are three main ways in which people speak when they are not saying the truth. He also discovered that the health of a person is likely to improve, not with the increased application of the emotion words such as joyful, happy, and sad, but with more use of the cognitive words such as understand, realize and know.

How Words Reveal Your Personality

Word clues tend to present a very non-invasive procedure to read people in an effective manner. If it is true that the eyes are the windows to the soul, then that can also imply that the words are the main gateway to the mind.

Basically, the words that we speak represent what we think. The closest that a person can get to be in a position of understanding the thoughts of other people will be based on how close he/she listens to the words they say or write. There are a couple of words that are used to reflect the behavioral features of the person who either wrote or spoke them.

These are what could be referred to as word clues. The word clues will tend to increase the probability of foretelling the behavioral features of people by analyzing the kind of words they picked when they wrote or spoke.

Just word clues alone are not capable of determining the personality traits of a person; however, they offer insights into the thought process of a person as well as the behavioral features and traits.

It is also very important to note that hypothesis can be developed entirely based on the main word clues, and then tested by using extra information that has been elicited from either the person or a corroboration with a third party.

The brain of a human being has been designed to work in a very efficient manner. Each time we think, we only put into use the nouns and verbs. Adverbs, adjectives, and other components of a speech are usually added during the transformation of thoughts into written or spoken language. The words that we add tend to reflect who we are and our thoughts.

Normally, a basic sentence will be made up of a verb and a subject. A simple sentence, such as "I walked" is made up of the pronoun "I," which is the main subject, as well as the word "walked," which is the main verb. Any words that are added to this kind of basic structure of a sentence can be used to modify either the quality of the noun or the action of the main verb. These kinds of modifications tend to offer clues to the behavioral and personality features of either the writer or the speaker.

Word clues also provide the observers with an opportunity to make guesses or hypotheses that pertains to the behavioral features of other people. In the sentence "I quickly ran," for instance, the word clue "quickly" is used to introduce a sense of urgency, although it fails to offer the reason for the urgency.

A person might be forced to quickly run since he is late for some business or maybe just anticipating lateness to the said commitment. Those who are conscientious view themselves as reliable and would usually try not to be late for an appointment.

Those who desire to be on time, at all the times, tend to give much respect to the social norms, and would always want to live to the expectations of other people.

Individuals who have this kind of behavioral feature have also been discovered to make the best workers since they will not desire to disappoint their bosses. One of the reasons why people quickly walk or run is when they encounter general threats.

This can be so common when walking through a neighborhood that has a bad name. When there is impending bad weather, a global threat might be seen. Running fast to avoid an impending thunderstorm tend to lower the danger of a lightning strike or even being rained on. People might go ahead and add the word quickly for some reasons, but there is usually a reason for the choices that they make. Word clues tend to present some noninvasive procedure to read people without their knowledge efficiently.

Here are some of the word clues that offer certain insights into the behavioral features of people each time they speak.

I earned another honorary degree.

The word clue in this sentence is "another." It is used to give a notion that the speaker has earned more than one previous honorary degrees. The person wanted to prove to others that he/she has earned at least one honorary degree.

It is a smart way of bolstering the self-image of a person. The speaker may require the admiration of others to be able to show his/her self-esteem. Professional observers could exploit this kind of vulnerability by using flattery and comments that can help in enhancing the ego of the speaker.

I have worked so hard to achieve my goal.

The word clue in this sentence is "hard." It suggests that the speaker values goals that appear so hard to achieve. The sentence might also indicate that the goals that the person has made could be more difficult to achieve than the goals that he usually attempts to achieve.

The word clue in this sentence also offers other suggestions. It also shows that the speaker can defer gratification or strongly believes that dedication and hard work tend to produce a better result.

A job seeker that has the following characteristics stands higher chances of getting a job because the character traits could be attractive to the employers. It is because this is a kind of individual who would accept challenges and have the determination to be able to finish up tasks in a successful way.

I patiently sat through the public lecture forum.

The word clue in this sentence is "patiently'. It can be used in many hypotheses. It could mean that the person could have been bored with the public lecture forum. Perhaps the person was forced to talk on the phone or even use the restroom.

No matter the kind of reason, the person has evidently preoccupied with other things apart from the main contents of the public lecture forum. Someone who patiently waits for a break before leaving a forum or a room is someone who obeys the social etiquette and norms.

A person whose phone rings and gets up immediately and leaves the room shows that they do not have strong rigid for the social boundaries. Those who have social barriers stand higher chances of getting job opportunities because they not only respect the authorities but also follow the rules to the later.

Employers will analyze the characters of these people by listening to the kind of speeches that they offer.

On the other hand, someone who fails to follow the social conventions would stand a chance of getting a job that needs novel thinking.

Someone who has the predisposition to act outside the social norms would make a good spy as opposed to someone who is disposed to follow the social conventions. This is because spies are usually asked to violate the social norms on a routine.

I opted to purchase that model.

The word clue in this sentence is "opted." It shows that the person weighs a few options before deciding to make the final purchase. At times, they could have struggled to some extent before making the final decision to buy what they wanted.

The behavior trait showcased here is that this is a person who thinks through making the decision to buy something. The word "opted" can also be used to show that this person is not likely to be impulsive.

Someone impulsive would likely use words such as "I just purchased that model". The word clue in this second sentence is "just" and suggests that the person just purchased the item without giving it much though.

Based on the first-word clue of "opted," the listener can go ahead and develop a hypothesis that the speaker is an introvert. Introverts are the type of people who usually think before they decide. However, they tend to carefully weigh on each of the options that they have before giving their views and decision. Introverts, on the other hand, tend to be more impulsive.

The use of the verb "opted" does not identify the speaker as an introvert in a positive manner, but it seeks to offer an indication that the person could be an introvert.

A detailed personality test needs a more definitive psychological assessment. However, an observer is still able to exploit a person if he is aware that the person tends towards the side of introversion and extroversion.

Extroverts are the kind of people who would get their energy from spending time with other people and look for stimulation from their surroundings.

They also tend to speak spontaneously without having a second thought and use the trial and error methods more confidently. The introverts, on the other hand, tend to expend the energy that they got when they socially engage and seek some lonely time to perform other errands.

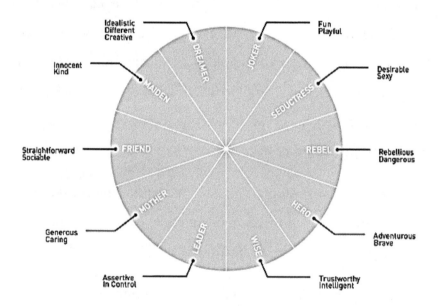

Chapter 6:

Understanding Various Types of

Personalities

Coming to the realization that certain facets of our personalities are deeply involved at different degrees on a daily basis – at home, play, or work – is one thing. Getting the best way of using that particular knowledge is another thing. Identifying various personality traits is very important. It can help us improve our relationships, exert our influences, attain success, and communicate in a more effective way.

Have you ever felt that you are experiencing some hard time speaking to your colleagues or manager? There could be many reasons behind this. You could be feeling that your colleagues are obnoxious and inappropriate, or maybe your manager might have set very high expectations.

The reason to all these does not matter but getting to understand that we human beings are genetically and inherently different, and we have been created to think differently is one of the primary keys to a conducive work environment.

When we understand those that are around us, we will be able to become more business leaders, entrepreneurs, friendly workmates, and business leaders.

Defining Personality Types

Personality type can be best defined as the psychological grouping of various individuals that have special behavioral tendencies. Bot h industrial and organizational psychologists use science to study the behavior of other human beings in their workplaces.

These psychologists are able to use personality tests to give people roles in various parts of companies and organizations entirely based on personality scores and behavioral traits.

For a very long time, psychologists have been exploring the personality type theory since Jung introduced the concept back in the 1910s. Jung was able to identify four basic functions that included:

- Sensing – S
- Intuiting – N
- Thinking – T
- Functioning – F

These basic functions were identified either in the internal or external worlds. Jung, who was a Swiss psychotherapist/psychiatrist, used 8 cognitive processes that were displayed as either a capital letter for the process and a small letter to show the orientation.

The three main preference areas that Jung introduced were dichotomous, implying that they were bipolar dimensions where each pole was used to represent a different preference. The psychiatrist also proposed that one of the four mentioned functions must be dominant in a person.

It could either be a function of judging or a role of perception. A researcher and a practitioner of Jung's theory, Isabel Briggs Myers proposed to see the judging and perceiving relationship as a fourth dichotomy that appeared to influence the personality type.

In the theory of Myers Briggs, for each pair, you will incline your preferences to one style more than the other. Jung also allowed a middle group where an equal balance of the two can be liked. The letters that are linked to your preferences will be combined to get a Myers Briggs personality type. Having preferences for E, S, T, and J, for instance, will offer a personality type of ESTJ.

From that analysis, here are the four main personality types that people have been divided into.

The Playfuls – Basically, these are loud, funny, enthusiastic, and energetic extroverts who like speaking to people. These people are best at socializing and networking. In addition to that, the playfuls are forgiving, unorganized, and get distracted easily. They are also creative, full of ideas, and tend to work very fast.

The Peaceful – As the title puts it clearly, these are the kind of people who spend time observing and maintaining peace and order. But apart from keeping peace and order, the peaceful are also diplomatic, patient, and easy going. They always try to avoid any possible confrontation with others. These people are also very grounded and are also emotionally stable. They tend to balance out the companies that are fast-paced or on the move, and they can also build a great working team.

The Powerful – As the title suggests, these kinds of people are authoritative. However, apart from the authoritative presence that they showcase, these people are also very productive, do not easily give up, take control, decisive, work hard to attain all their goals and objectives and are always attempting to get to the main point.

The Précises – The précises people who are precise to details. In short, they greatly value compliance, order, and structure. They are usually organized and are strong perfectionists when it comes to following the procedures. They are the kind of people who put work before play and will just stop working when they have ensured that everything is in the right order.

To be able to run an engaging and successful business, all the personality types should be observed. Each of the personality types tends to utilize different weaknesses and strengths and should be consistently valued. As noted from the list of four personality types, there are some people who are good at offering insights like the peaceful. There are also others that offer critical thinking, planning, and analysis like the Precises.

Interacting with each Personality Type

The playfuls will usually want some attention, fondness, and approval

The powerfuls, on the other hand, will prefer loyalty, credit and some appreciation

The peaceful will look for value, respect, as well as harmony between those who are working at the same workstation

Précises typically prefer sensitivity, space to work alone, and a quiet environment

Case Study: Analyzing the Précises and Playful

While précises prefer working in quiet environments, the playful like attention. The also précises introverts while the playful are extroverts. This shows that these two personalities are opposite of each other.

One of the best ways of working with introverts is to offer them the space they need to work. It is also imperative to note that small talk may not be so productive when it comes to working with them.

The playful, who are just extroverts, are the exact opposite of the précises. They enjoy being in the company of other people. Generally, the playful will feel so comfortable making eye-to-eye contact when they are speaking to a person. Extroverts, on the other hand, will always want to think that they belong to a team. They also want it to be known that their hard work is not going to waste. They like to socialize, and when they are given social freedom during work hours greatly assist them to be productive and to prioritize better.

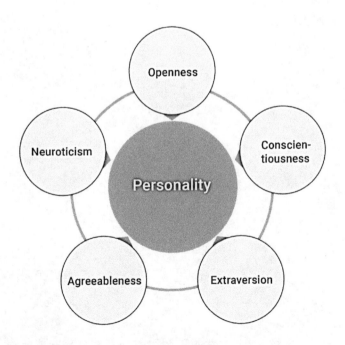

Manipulation Tips And Tricks

Conclusion

Understanding the human mind is one of the most complex wide varieties of wirings of the past coined together with the chemical and physical inclinations of the present. Psychology is the study of the human brain.

However, it extends way past the dissection of loads of other misleading information that is trapped in our heads. Essentially, it is a study of what makes us, human beings, tick as species and individuals.

This e-book is meant to show the main facets of a human being and how all these works together to make a person function. The e-book has been divided into various aspects of human psychology that includes decision-making, personality, emotions, behavior, relationships, as well as morality.

To understand all that makes a person wholly human and think in a certain way is to have mastered psychological sleight of hand, and this e-book will serve as a significant step to understanding that magic trick.

How human beings behave and think is one of the most unendingly interesting studies. It shows how elegant and simple and, to some extent, mysteries and complicated human beings are.

Some of the topics that have been covered in this eBook will try as much as possible to make the whole process of analyzing human beings so easy. The eBook talks about analyzing people through the nonverbal of the palms and the hands. Ways of detecting lies in people have also been discussed in the eBook, as well as how to analyze people who are in love and dating.

CPSIA information can be obtained
at www.ICGtesting.com
Printed in the USA
BVHW011159170521
607543BV00007B/1079